21ST CENTURY HEALING

BOB BENDYKOWSKI

BALBOA.PRESS
A DIVISION OF HAY HOUSE

Balboa Press books may be ordered through booksellers or by contacting:

Balboa Press
A Division of Hay House
1663 Liberty Drive
Bloomington, IN 47403
www.balboapress.com
1 (877) 407-4847

Because of the dynamic nature of the Internet, any web addresses or links contained in this book may have changed since publication and may no longer be valid. The views expressed in this work are solely those of the author and do not necessarily reflect the views of the publisher, and the publisher hereby disclaims any responsibility for them.

The author of this book does not dispense medical advice or prescribe the use of any technique as a form of treatment for physical, emotional, or medical problems without the advice of a physician, either directly or indirectly. The intent of the author is only to offer information of a general nature to help you in your quest for emotional and spiritual well-being. In the event you use any of the information in this book for yourself, which is your constitutional right, the author and the publisher assume no responsibility for your actions.

Any people depicted in stock imagery provided by Getty Images are models, and such images are being used for illustrative purposes only. Certain stock imagery © Getty Images.

Print information available on the last page.

ISBN: 978-1-9822-5121-5 (sc)
ISBN: 978-1-9822-5169-7 (e)

Balboa Press rev. date: 08/11/2020

IT IS PART OF THE EVOLUTIONARY PLAN FOR HUMANS TO
ASSIST OR TAKE OVER THE WORK OF ANGELS IN A VARIETY
OF WAYS. HEALING, FOR INSTANCE, WILL ONE DAY BE
PERFORMED BY CAREFULLY TRAINED PRIESTS WHO WILL
SUMMON AND DIRECT ANGELIC FORCES TO REPAIR HUMAN
BODIES, INSTEAD OF USING MEDICINES OR SURGERY.
Robert Leichtman & Carl Japikse: Working With Angels
Enthea Press, 1992

CONTENTS

AUTHOR'S INTRODUCTION

THE GENSIS OF MY QUEST FOR HEALING

This book contains knowledge that has been lost for over twenty centuries. It is important that the reader know how this information was obtained so that he or she can personally judge its validity. To do this requires some autobiographical input from the author. I promise it will be as brief as possible.

My early childhood was relatively uneventful. I did however experience all five of the diseases associated with that period including the most serious, scarlet fever. Today I probably would be called a sickly child, but the discomfort I had left me with a fully trained immune system which has protected me through the rest of my life.

I always seemed to know where I was going. At age eleven my uncle Matt who was living with us bought a small grand piano and a home study course to learn how to play. Shortly thereafter I was looking through the books and soon displayed both interest and talent. I took lessons from a neighborhood teacher for a while but by the time I entered high school I was learning by myself.

From high school I entered a local university; however, after two years of mostly non-musical classes I moved to the Conservatory. Here I progressed so rapidly that I was hired to teach there after graduation. I stayed at the conservatory for ten years. Half way through my tenure I sprained my left ankle stepping on some broken concrete. Instead of going to a doctor I bought a cane and hobbled around until the condition healed by itself.

But music was not to be my life's work. While my musical performance was very good my teaching was only acceptable. I left the conservatory on a high note by playing a full solo recital. The second half of the program was devoted to a single composition, the Sonata in

B minor by Franz Liszt, a thirty minute tour de force rarely performed live today. I started playing and, in what seemed like a few minutes, completed the entire composition. It was only many years later that I learned that, in a former life, I had actually composed this work.

In need of employment I applied at General Electric Medical Systems and was promptly hired to be an inspector of incoming materials. Obviously, my experience as a classical musician and teacher was considered valuable for the manufacturing of X-ray tubes. I spent twenty-nine years at GE moving from mechanical inspection to electrical inspection to electronics technician to lead technician of a small test area. All this was accomplished by home courses in electronics, the same way I learned piano.

During my time at GE my old ankle injury started to flare up. It was especially bad on Monday mornings after a weekend of puttering around on household projects; however, I did notice that my discomfort diminished as I moved around. Then I (accidently?) discovered a magazine article about Homeopathy and started investigating it for a remedy for my ankle. I found my remedy to be Rhus Tox which is prepared from poison ivy—its description fit my symptoms exactly. I obtained some of the pills and one Sunday night I popped three of them under my tongue and climbed into bed. In about ten minutes I experienced a severe attack of "pins and needles" in my sore ankle. The tingling soon faded away and so did I. The next morning my ankle was almost completely healed and has remained healed to this day.

This incident was the starting point for my research into healing, a quest to last for the rest of my life. I continued to study Homeopathy for a number of years and during that time I ran across a book on Radionics. Not as well known as Homeopathy, Radionics can be defined as "instrument assisted distant healing." It employs specially designed electronic devices to direct remedies to patients. The most important thing I learned from my study of Radionics was dowsing, the ancient method of finding water, which was adapted in this system to questioning the Universe for information. This procedure consists in verbalizing a question and using a pendulum and a previously established code to elicit a "yes" or "no" answer. The questions must be carefully thought out. For example: "Does the sun rise in the East?" The pendulum would swing to NO because the sun does not rise at all. Rephrasing: "Does the sun appear to rise in the East?" would result in a "YES." Dowsing provides clearer information than that channeled by mediums.

In this materialistic age there is no logical explanation for dowsing. But for me, after about six months of working with a pendulum, I got the distinct impression that my questions were being answered by someone instead of being pulled out of thin air. Research in another book led me to the Theosophical Society, one of a few groups safeguarding what is known as the "Ancient Wisdom" or the "Perennial Philosophy," which is information about the creation of the Universe and the unfolding of life on Earth. I learned about the spiritual hierarchy guiding what I call Project Earth and that the vast majority of humans have Mentors who, like faculty advisors in college, guide their Proteges with dreams, intuition, and conscience. Perhaps this is the origin of Guardian Angels.

I have never seen a ghost. I have never heard voices from nowhere. I have never had any unexplainable experiences. My explanation is not that these things do not exist, but that they never happen to me because of the scientific nature of my quest. Since the 18th century doctors have been dissecting human vehicles trying to find out how they work. Today there are powerful microscopes and other instruments which probe flesh and blood seeking causes for disease. But these devices and procedures will never detect the underlying invisible energies which create and sustain physical bodies. Albert Einstein proved that matter is condensed energy. But if you condense faulty energy you end up with faulty matter. This book examines the energy patterns of the human vehicle in a scientific manner by extracting information from the Beings who were involved in its creation and are still involved in its perfection. All of the material presented here has been verified as accurate by my own Mentor who has been known through the ages as Raphael. And this is the same knowledge which was taught in the Mystery Schools whose outstanding student is still well known to this day, Jesus Christ!

This then is the quest I ventured on about forty years ago:

TO DISCOVER HOW HEALING WORKS AND
HOW TO APPLY IT IN THE 21st CENTURY

PROLOGUE

Go back in time about 2000 years. In the Middle East an itinerant preacher and healer journeys from village to village helping the inhabitants with their problems both spiritual and physical. Being more highly evolved than the common man he is very successful in his chosen field. Look closely, for he is followed by an assistant pulling a cart filled with assorted equipment and supplies.

The preacher/healer enters a village and the people crowd around him. Many are seeking healing. For simple diseases he passes out bottles of pills from the cart. More complicated conditions require poking and prodding with strange looking instruments. For extreme conditions the healer uses sharp little knives to excise the offending flesh.

OOPS! I HAVE MIXED UP MY TIMELINES!

Healing was much simpler 20 centuries ago. Water was pure and food was simple. The air was clean and held only the Sun's beneficial rays. Diseases were a part of life, but not as varied and as serious as those we have today. The quest for the underlying cause of diseases is as old as the first sick person. But medical science really started to blossom about the middle of the 18th century. Invention of the microscope triggered a search for new ways to invade the human vehicle in order to locate, and then eradicate, whatever was responsible for the outward symptoms of the disease. However, in spite of tremendous advancements in technology, diseases such as cancer still demand huge monetary investments without any promise of successful and lasting cures.

What is needed is a revival of an old technology, healing, which works by correcting the faulty energetic patterns underlying all disease symptoms. What is needed is a re-discovery of the information and techniques taught in the Mystery Schools thousands of years ago, the schools attended by our itinerant healer. Perhaps then the following scenario will become common:

Fast forward fifty years. A new patient enters the doctor's offices and is handed a questionnaire. The first question is:

HAVE YOU CONSULTED A HEALER?

CHAPTER ONE
ANGELS

Angel: A spirit being believed to act as an attendant, agent, or messenger of God.

FOR THOSE WHO BELIEVE, NO PROOF IS NECESSARY. FOR THOSE WHO DON'T BELIEVE, NO PROOF IS POSSIBLE.
STUART CHASE

IN THE BEGINNING.........

Many people do not believe in angels because they can't see them. The five senses of the human vehicle are designed to work only in the Earth's environment and are therefore set for low frequency operation. Some people, known as clairvoyants, can see many things outside the average person's range, but this can become problematic if it cannot be controlled during daily life. The clairvoyant most familiar to the general public was Sylvia Browne who appeared frequently on television.

It would be very arrogant to think that there are no sentient beings between God and humanity. Therefore, I now submit my findings and thoughts about the Creation of the Cosmos in which we exist, and its many unseen inhabitants.

A study of Theosophy shows that there are periods of creation called Manvantaras, and periods of rest called Pralayas. My source informs me that we are six billion earth years into a manvantara expected to last fifteen billion earth years. Of course, this has absolutely no practical value, but for now we need not fear collapse of our solar system. Also, we have no way of determining how many manvantaras preceded the current one. My indication is that some of the stuff created during a manvantara does not dematerialize during the pralayas and remains as a starting point for the next round of creation. If that is true the "Big-Bang" theory becomes implausible.

The beginning of the Bible, Genesis, states that "God created heaven and earth," and goes on with "God said 'Let there be light!' "Let us examine an ancient thought and two modern theories which may throw some light on the start of the current manvantara.

1.
TAO IS A WHIRLING EMPTINESS,
YET WHEN USED IT CANNOT BE EXHAUSTED.
OUT OF THIS MYSTERIOUS WELL
FLOWS EVERYTHING IN EXISTENCE.....
SOMETHING IS THERE, HIDDEN IN THE DEEP!
BUT I DO NOT KNOW WHOSE CHILD IT IS—
IT CAME EVEN BEFORE GOD.
The Tao te Ching of Lao Tzu
Translated by Brian Browne Walker
St. Martin's Griffin Edition: December 1996

2.
Dark matter is a hypothetical form of matter that is thought to account for approximately 85% of the matter in the universe, and about a quarter of its total energy density. The majority of dark matter is thought to be non-baryonic in nature, possibly being composed of some as-yet undiscovered subatomic particles.

Wikipedia

3.
Zero Point Field and Non-Locality – Mantak Chia

The zero point field is a repository of all fields and all ground energy states and all virtual particles-a field of fields. Every exchange of every virtual particle radiates energy. If you add up all the particles of all varieties constantly popping in and out of being, you come up with a vast, inexhaustible energy source.

www.mantakchia.com/zero-point-field-and-non-locality

A careful reading of these three descriptions shows an uncanny similarity in their content. My indication is that the three different names are all being applied to exactly the same phenomenon, seemingly empty space!

Let's go back to Genesis Chapter One. We now have to deal with thousands of years of translations and mis-translations and hundreds of years of editing and mis-editing. However, most editions of the Bible agree that God's creation of the sea and the land came before "Let there be Light!" What if that Light was not the solar light we assume it to be. What if that Light was the light of enlightenment, or of awakening. Upon awakening what is the first thing we see before our eyes can focus—light. And only after light can we then recognize forms. Perhaps our Creator has His(?) own Circadian rhythm of billions of years and at the end of a pralaya awakes to the remnants of His last manvantara.

If there is one important idea to be taken from this brief description of the beginning of creation is that all that exists in the entire Cosmos began as thoughts in the mind of God and was fabricated from God-stuff.

Perhaps Herbert Spencer had the right idea when he described God as a mind:

GOD IS INFINITE INTELLIGENCE,
INFINITELY DIVERSIFIED THROUGH
INFINITE TIME AND INFINITE SPACE,
MANIFESTING THROUGH AN
INFINITUDE OF EVER-EVOLVING INDIVIDUALITIES.

CREATION BEGINS

About three thousand years ago a very wise individual walked on Earth. His name was Hermes Trismegistus, thrice wise Hermes. My indication is that Hermes was an incarnation of the ascended Master Isolt. Hermes' basic teachings from ancient Egypt and Greece have been compiled in a slender volume known as the Kybalion. Here we will only consider his most famous saying:

AS ABOVE, SO BELOW; AS BELOW, SO ABOVE.

This simple statement tells us that developments on Earth often imitate the organization and procedures of the spirit plane. With that idea in mind let us consider God to be an engineer instead of a magistrate.

God operates at the highest possible frequency; therefore, anything he creates must be of lower frequency than himself. There are millions of stars in the Cosmos, so let us assume that he started making them. He gathered some of his dark matter into a ball and squeezed it tightly. Because of the material's high frequency this compaction caused its frequency to slow down, and the friction of the particles produced both heat and light. A star was born!

What about the planets and other objects now in space? Stars such as our sun exist in time and will eventually die out or explode resulting in planets and space debris. After about 300 manvantaras God decided that he needed help with his creative endeavors. After much thought He brought forth seven entities known in the Ancient Wisdom as Dhyani-Chohans who were equipped with powers only slightly less than God himself. These powerful beings were charged with the evolution of the Cosmos. To do this efficiently they constructed the Great Central Sun, a mechanism which automatically converts the Chief Engineer's thoughts into reality. And, being good managers, they select only those thoughts which contribute to the progress of evolution.

To assist in this work the Dhyani-Chohans created ten on-site supervisors called Kosmocratores who oversee operations in the field. These were the entities who prepared Earth's solar system for what I have called Project Earth, but the number of entities assisting them can only be imagined.

Here then is a partial listing of the spirit hierarchy involved in Project Earth.

THE COSMIC PLANE

THE WEB OF CONSCIOUSNESS, ENERGY,
AND MATTER—THE TAO
THE DHYANI-CHOHANS
THE GREAT CENTRAL SUN
THE KOSMOCRATORES

EARTH'S SOLAR SYSTEM

1. THE SILENT WATCHERS
2. KUAN YIN—THE SOLAR LOGOS
3. KRISHNA: MAEVE, ISOLT, ISHTAR
4. LAKSHMI: SANAT KUMARA, KUTHUMI, KALI
5. ISIS: LIGH, OONAGH, MAITREYA
6. MICHAEL: RAPHAEL, GABRIEL, AINE
7. PHYSICAL MATTER—EARTH AND LIFEFORMS

The Silent Watchers can be considered the managers of the Project. They are constantly adjusting conditions on Earth. The weather in its many manifestations, the structure of the earth, the general health of all living things, and the numbers and actions of the human inhabitants, especially those who wield influence over the general population—all these things are carefully monitored and fine tuned to keep the Project on track. The Solar Logos is the CEO of the Project, reporting to the

Silent Watchers and conveying their instructions to the workers in the field.

The main body of these spirit workers is represented by the supervisors and their assistants in levels 3 through 6. There are about `17,000 invisible entities aiding all lifeforms on Earth, of which 12,000 are dedicated to humans. Five thousand of these have earned the right to be designated Spirit Doctors. These SD's are critical to healing because souls encased in human vehicles are not able to adequately control the high frequency energies required to produce the desired results. This was true even of Master Jesus Christ.

But, you say, thousands of people are dying every day and their relatives and friends are grief stricken, property is destroyed by bad weather and wars, and in general everything seems to be going to Hell. Why don't these powerful Silent Watchers make things a little easier for their Proteges?

While that seems to be true, Project Earth is both an experiment in evolution and a university for training souls by experiences in low frequency flesh and blood vehicles. This includes dealing with both the joys and, unfortunately, the sorrows of such an existence. And, when we look at the scope and purpose of the Project, we come to realize that in death our loved ones go from strife to peace, rest, and a new beginning. The overall scenario was probably best understood by William Shakespeare:

ALL THE WORLD'S A STAGE, AND ALL
THE MEN AND WOMEN MERELY
PLAYERS; THEY HAVE THEIR EXITS
AND THEIR ENTRANCES, AND
ONE MAN IN HIS TIME PLAYS MANY PARTS.....

PROJECT EARTH

Across the Cosmos there are currently eight large scale projects dealing with the development of low frequency life forms. Seven of these are concerned only with flora and fauna. Project Earth is unique because its main purpose is to provide a low frequency, that is flesh and blood, experience to evolving souls. To accomplish this required not only the development of a suitable vehicle, but also an environment in which such vehicles could grow and mature gradually. For this the Dhyani-Chohans conceived and launched Project Earth.

The Project was designed to require about four billion earth years. The first billion was spent searching the Cosmos for the best solar system; then all the planets in that system were tested with life forms from the other Cosmic projects. Having selected the most suitable planet, called Earth, they laid out the human vehicle's development. This requires seven epochs, or Root Races, until the desired level of perfection is achieved. We are presently blending into the Fifth Root Race.

Here then is the approximate timeline in years of Project Earth:

-400,000,000: Earth selected as an R&D location. Sun reprogramming initiated. Emanations from all the other planets adjusted to agree with and support the Sun's output. Thus, Mars became the "Red Planet," and the others were set to the colors of the rainbow.

-300,000,000: Plant and animal lifeforms transferred from other star systems to start development of a suitable atmosphere. The unicorn and other now legendary animals were brought to Earth at this time but were not able to adapt to the environment.

-200,000,000: Programming of the Sun continues. Magnetic field added to the Earth to stir and evenly distribute the Sun's energies. Plants and animals thriving.

-100,000,000: Dinosaurs and other large lifeforms develop.

-13,000,000: First Root Race: Souls without vehicles, the first sentient beings move into their new home.

-10,000,000: Second Root Race: Flesh and blood vehicles being developed. Sun's output undergoes fine tuning. Schumann Resonance Pulses added to regulate plant and animal growth on Earth. This signaled the end of the dinosaurs.

-8,000,000:	The age of the caveman. Dinosaurs dying out.
-7,500,000:	The Flood: Noah and eight others survive. Of course, the flood did did not encompass the entire Earth and there were many humans left alive on other continents.
-7,000,000:	The Third Root Race. Lemuria thriving.
-6,000,000:	Engineers from Sirius arrive to assist in the development of the human vehicle. Sun programming completed.
-5,000,000:	Engineers from Pleiades and Betelgeuse arrive. Human vehicle development continues.
-2,000,000:	Fourth Root Race. Homo sapiens. Atlantis thriving.
-1,000,000:	Homo sapiens sapiens. The Golden Age begins.
-35,000:	Hinduism arises.
-12,500:	Cataclysm and a new beginning! Tilting of the Earth results in the changing seasons and more arable land for agriculture.
-12,000:	Mystery Schools are established in Africa (3) and China (4).
-10,000:	Recorded history begins.

When we attend a play we expect to have one or more intermissions. These allow the stagehands to reset the stage for the next act. Project Earth is a very largescale drama being played out on a very large stage. To date there have been two re-settings since the curtain was raised: Noah's flood and the Cataclysm twelve thousand five hundred years ago. Through the centuries there have been many minor resets caused by weather, fire, earthquakes, disease, war--and the list goes on. Although these challenges will continue to test and strengthen humanity, my indication is that a complete cataclysm will not occur for another three thousand years. And this will usher in the Seventh, and last, Root Race.

Note: The Sun is the source of all creative energies. The Earth's magnetic field was added to stir and evenly distribute the Sun's energies in the atmosphere. It also acts as an unlimited source of Chi. The Schumann Resonance was put in place to regulate plant and animal growth. It signaled the end of the dinosaurs.

As these words are being written the pandemic of Corona Virus is resetting the stage for the next act of Project Earth. My indication is that this Virus will become endemic and is being introduced to replace measles, mumps, and all the other common childhood diseases intended to educate the human immune system. This virus will be totally resistant to vaccination.

CHAPTER TWO

RAINBOWS

Rainbow: An arch of colors formed in the sky in certain circumstances, caused by the refraction and dispersion of the sun's light by rain or other water droplets in the atmosphere.

"I HAVE SET MY BOW IN THE CLOUDS, AND IT SHALL SERVE AS A SIGN OF THE COVENANT BETWEEN ME AND THE EARTH."
THE TORAH: GENESIS 9:13

THE SUN—THE SOURCE OF THE EARTH'S BIOSPHERE

Biosphere: The regions of the surface, atmosphere, and hydrosphere of the Earth occupied by living organisms.

Inayat Kahn tells a Hindu story of a fish who went to a queen and asked:

"I have always heard about the sea, but what is the sea? Where is it?" The queen fish explained: "You live, move, and have your being in the sea. The sea is within you and without you, and you are made of the sea, and you will end in sea.
The sea surrounds you as your own being."

Just as the sea supplies all the necessities for the life of its inhabitants, so the Sun generates and supplies all the intelligence and energies necessary to create and maintain life in the Earth's biosphere. As noted earlier there are seven other evolutionary projects in the Cosmos developing flora and fauna lifeforms.

But because of the covenant between God, speaking through Krishna, and Noah after the flood, only Earth's sunlight produces a rainbow when refracted.

Research into the mystery of the rainbow resulted in this solution: The white of sunlight consists of neutral photons which produce warmth upon striking solid matter. But the photon stream also acts as a carrier wave for twenty-three units of transcendental information and energy. Further lengthy research resulted in this breakdown of the solar components:

COLOR	PROGRAMS	ETHERS	ENERGIES
Violet	Apana	Air	
Indigo	Prana		Chi
Blue	Iana	Fire	Fohat
Green	Samana		Daed
Yellow	Upana		Klimi
Orange	Ridana	Earth	Kundalini
Red	Vyana	Water	

COLORS: The seven color bands are the carrier waves for all solar programs and energies. The colors themselves are used to balance and stabilize the mental and emotional aspects of the human personality. For example, a person who is very angry might well be described as "seeing red," and a sad person feeling "blue."

PROGRAMS: Three of the listed operating programs are stored in the human matrices. These instruction sets supply the INTELLIGENCE needed to construct and maintain the human vehicle. All the raw materials for this process are supplied by the Sun either directly or indirectly by food and water. The direct creative forces from the Sun cannot be turned off but are balanced by the INTELLIGENCE in the programs. If this INTELLIGENCE is compromised the Sun will keep on doing what it was designed to do and anomalies, irregularities, and malfunctions will develop in the flesh and blood vehicle. As noted earlier the Schumann Resonance controls the Sun's energies by interrupting their flow about eight times a second; our life is like a movie, one frame at a time.

ETHERS: The four ethers are energies which condense to fabricate flesh and blood lifeforms:

> The Earth Ether condenses to create bone. This process
> is controlled by the Energy Kundalini.
> The Air and Water Ethers condense to create fluids.
> This process is controlled by the energy Fohat.
> The Earth, Air, and Water Ethers condense to create
> soft tissue. This process is controlled by the energy
> Klimi.
> The Fire Ether integrates and shapes the other Ethers
> into the appropriate Physical configurations.

ENERGIES: Chi is the energy of life which keeps all the components of the human vehicle active and functioning. Daed only comes into action when Chi is completely used up and dissolution of the lifeless body or of an abnormal growth is required.

CHAPTER THREE

COMPUTERS

This chapter could not have been written fifty years ago.
This chapter was written to supersede
the mystic mumbo-jumbo
which has obscured the healing
process for thousands of years.
This chapter had to wait for the
technology on Earth to progress
sufficiently so that the technology
used to create the human
vehicle could be understood and be used to heal it.

Computer: An electronic device for
storing and processing data,
normally in binary form, according
to instructions given to it in
a variable program.

MAN IS STILL THE MOST EXTRAORDINARY COMPUTER OF ALL.
John F. Kennedy

Around 1500 AD Leonardo de Vinci published a drawing for a flying machine. It was never constructed because the technology was not available to produce it. In the late 1800's Jules Verne described a vessel for sailing under water. It took about fifty years for the technology to catch up. In the first Star Trek series Captain Kirk used a small hand held device to communicate with the Enterprise. Unfortunately, this technology was available. Robotic machines are becoming commonplace in industry, but the development of a true android is still far in the future; however, in literature, Commander Data in Star Trek, the Next Generation, comes pretty close.

As with most literary heroes Data has a flaw, a lack of emotions. His brain is filled with the all knowledge available at the time and still has plenty room to spare; and he can make the correct decisions when he is in command. Physically, Data is stronger than any man and his life span is indeterminant. But because of the absence of the emotion Integrated Circuit (IC) Data realizes he will never become human. (Note: He does get this IC in one of the full-length movies.)

In several episodes Data is damaged and is either self-repaired or restored by the technical expertise of his human comrades. We might consider Data to be a living computer who will die only when his nuclear power unit fails completely.

Medical science has had a difficult time deciding when a human being is really dead. No pulse and no breath, the person is dead; no response to stimulation, the person is dead; no brainwave activity, the person is dead. Right now, there are human vehicles being kept alive artificially waiting for signs of recovery. But the true death of the vehicle occurs when the life force, soul or Protégé, departs never to return. And this can only be determined intuitively.

Looking at the timeline of Project Earth it took approximately five million years to progress from naked etheric beings (souls) to souls clothed in humanoid bodies. And after another seven million years the final design for Homo sapiens sapiens was approved by engineering. We are now in the field trial stage in order to detect and correct minor faults not found in the basic model. Here then is a very simplified list of the major components of a very complicated organism.

THE SOUL'S EARTHLY VEHICLE

THE SUBCONSCIOUS CPU:

DESTINY: LIFE PLAN, KARMA
HISTORY: FIVE INCARNATIONS
GENETIC: LINEAGE
CORE: CURRENT INCARNATION

MENTAL MATRIX EMOTIONAL
MATRIX ETHERIC MATRIX

THE ETHERIC CIRCUIT BOARD

DNA

THE VEHICLE'S ENERGY SYSTEMS:

MAJOR CHAKRAS
MINOR CHAKRAS
SPLEEN CHAKRA
MERIDIAN SYSTEM, NADIS
AURA

THE VEHICLE'S PHYSICAL SYSTEMS

What would it take today to build a human android?

Metal and plastic solids for bony structures.
Plastics of varying flexibility for soft tissues.
Liquids for lubrication; the need for a blood
substitute is questionable.
An everlasting lasting power source.
Miniature control IC's for mental, emotional, and
physical operations
An internal computer to manage all activities
Miles of signal carrying fiber optics
Artificial intelligence to make it function correctly

But why bother with all this when it has already been done by the engineers and technicians of Project Earth?

THE HUMAN COMPUTER IN A LARGE NUTSHELL

If your automobile breaks down you would not take it to a plumber for repairs. If a human vehicle breaks down the first attempt to repair it is a trip to the doctor. But today's medical system operates cosmetically by managing symptoms. This is like trying to get rid of an iceberg by chopping off the part that is above water. The human vehicle is so complicated that it can best be repaired by those who developed it in the first place.

Refer to "The Soul's Earthly Vehicle" above, and the Appendix.

The Physical Systems are the end product of everything listed above them. This is the flesh and blood vehicle which walks the Earth and is subjected to illness, accidents, weather, and all the good and the bad experiences which constitute human life. These Systems are constructed from seventeen Intelligence Modules (IM's) located in the Solar Plexus. The four Energy System IM's are also in the Solar Plexus along with the Cosmic Interface which identifies the Protégé and its location in the Universe.

The Subconscious CPU Intelligence Module is located in the medulla oblongata. This IM holds the History, Destiny, Genetic, and Core chips; it also has three chips which construct and manage the Mental, Emotional, and Etheric matrices. The matrices themselves hold the basic human thoughtforms but can accept new thoughtforms whether good or bad. These three matrices permeate and control the development of the entire vehicle.

DNA is the magic factory which converts the INTELLIGENCE written into the three matrices into a flesh and blood vehicle appropriate for the current incarnation.

How can a computer suffer a breakdown? There are three general circumstances which cause computer failure: aging, internal faults, and external damage.

Aging happens to everything; even the pyramids will eventually crumble to rubble, and the rubble will break down to sand. In our low frequency solar system wear and tear inevitably leads to total failure no matter how finely something is crafted. The human vehicle was designed to last for approximately ninety years. Unfortunately, because of current conditions on Earth the average person of that age is usually in no shape to really enjoy life. Internal, or INTRINSIC, faults and external, or EXTRINSIC, influences tend to foster both disease conditions and rapid aging. And trauma can end the vehicle's existence in a matter of minutes.

In the Seventh Root Race or epoch aging will stop at about thirty years and the decision to end an incarnation will be left to the Protégé. In the next chapter we will examine the main INTRINSIC and EXTRINSIC factors which disrupt the human vehicle and shorten its lifespan.

CHAPTER FOUR

HEALING

HEAL: THE PROCESS OF MAKING OR
BECOMING SOUND OR HEALTHY AGAIN.

THE SECRET OF HEALING IS TO CAUSE
HEALTH BY REMOVING THOSE
ARTIFICAL OBSTACLES WHICH IMPEDE
THE NATURAL FLOW OF LIFE.
Manley Palmer Hall

Studying this chapter at this time is not absolutely necessary to begin treatments. But it does supply information on FACTORS, the obstacles which interfere with the natural flow of solar energies. I recommend that you read it over briefly and return to it later for study.

ANALYZING THE PATIENT

JESHUA'S ABILITY TO TUNE INTO THE
SOUL OF THE PATIENT WAS
INCOMPARABLY BETTER THAN ANY
OTHER ESSENE. HE COULD HOLD
AN EXTENDED UNSPOKEN DIALOGUE WITH THE SOUL AT A
MULTIDIMENSIONAL LEVEL SO THAT IT
TOOK NO LINEAR TIME, AND
THIS GAVE HIM A CLEAR PICTURE OF HOW TO PROCEED.

. . . .

THE KEY TO A HEALING PROCESS IS TO
UNDERSTAND WHERE THE PROBLEM
COMES FROM, HOW FAR IT HAS SPREAD, AND HOW LONG
IT HAS BEEN IN THE PATIENT'S SYSTEM.
Stuart Wilson and Joanna Prentis:
The Magdalene Version: Secret Wisdom
from a Gnostic Mystery School
Ozark Mountain Publishing, 2012

The human vehicle is the most complicated living thing ever conceived—and it is still in the developmental stage. In the Theosophical Society time frame, measured in Root Races or epochs, Project Earth is transitioning into the Fifth of seven such periods. The current basic design of the human vehicle, with upgrades and fine tuning, is expected to last until the end of the Project.

When evaluated in terms of contemporary manufacturing practices we are presently in the field trial phase. Engineering has approved the basic design, homo sapiens sapiens, and many varieties, with their Protégés, have been delivered to planet Earth through the centuries. Project engineers are now evaluating feedback about their work in order to pinpoint design flaws and fine tune the flesh and blood mechanisms.

But the Project has hit a snag. Having strayed from their spiritual and energetic origins the ailing vehicles on Earth are attempting to repair themselves by manipulating their flesh and blood components with drugs and surgery. While this may seem to be successful with trauma and infection, true healing of slowly developing diseases will only take place by decontaminating and repairing the energetic structure which animates and sustains the dense physical body.

I SING THE BODY ELECTRIC
Walt Whitman

The human vehicle, when considered as a complete unit, is part of a circuit similar to a flashlight. The battery in the flashlight is the voltage source which, when in a closed circuit with the bulb, pushes current through the bulb (resistance) heating it until it glows. This illustrates the three basic components of a simple circuit: voltage, current, and resistance.

When applied to a human vehicle the physical body is the resistance. The voltage is the difference in electrical potential between Kundalini energy, from the Sun, and the Earth which is the ground for all electrical activity. The current is the magnetic energy from the Earth's molten iron core. This energy, which forms a field around the Earth, is known in Eastern spiritual and martial arts traditions as Chi or Qi. As this Chi flows through the human vehicle it carries with it all the components of sunlight necessary to construct, maintain, and repair it.

The resistance of the vehicle is the key factor in maintaining its health. In very rare cases the resistance decreases from its optimum value and Chi flow increases resulting in spontaneous human combustion. Usually the opposite happens—resistance increases and Chi flow decreases resulting in aging and the development of disease conditions. In order to heal the vehicle properly we must decontaminate it to reduce resistance and repair any leftover damage which might have occurred.

STRANDS, CLUSTERS, AND LOOPS

WE CAN MAKE HIGHLY SOPHISTICATED MEASUREMENTS THAT SHOW THAT WHENEVER THERE IS THE SLIGHTEST CHANGE IN ANY SYSTEM IN THE BODY, ALL OTHER SYSTEMS ARE SOMEHOW EFFECTED. NO LONGER CAN WE VIEW OUR BODY AS A COLLECTION OF SEPARATE ORGANS THROWN INTO A BAG IN WHICH A SPECIALIST CAN FIX ONE ORGAN WITHOUT AFFECTING THE OTHERS.
Itzhak Bentov: Stalking the Wild Pendulum

The major flaw in the current vehicle's design is its perfect and intricate complexity! The human body has approximately 900 feedback loops which are constantly making adjustments to optimize its structure and function. These loops also interact with each other causing the resulting configuration impossible to analyze except by the Spirit Engineers who originally designed it. Since this basic design was intended to last through the Seventh Root Race it must be assumed to be essentially perfect and any faults which disrupt it, if not caused by Life Plan or Karma algorithms, are due to minor design flaws or by factors internal or external to the entity. Such a finely tuned life form is very susceptible to disruptions which impinge upon it, and even the smallest disruption can trigger a cascade effect which can distort normal energy patterns. These initial disruptions can originate in the Protégé's current life on Earth or can often be traced back to previous incarnations.

An initial unhealed disruption sends a fault signal through the vehicle's energetic infrastructure randomly impairing other systems or components. This process eventually produces a strand of faults scattered through the mental, emotional, and etheric matrices.

Sometimes randomly, but often due to the demands of the Protégé's Karma or Life Plan, a simple energy strand will branch out and produce a cluster of faults effecting several physical systems. And in the worst case scenario a strand from the cluster will find its way back to the site of the initial disruption. The result is the formation of a self-sustaining feedback loop eventually gaining enough strength to surface as overt symptoms in the physical vehicle. The circular nature of the loop also explains how diseases might travel to and effect systems distant from the initial point of diagnosis. The development of multiple clusters and loops interferes internally with information processing and externally with the body's absorption of healing energies from the Sun. They are the main cause of aging.

By the time of the Seventh Root Race these disease inducing faults will have been redesigned out of the human vehicle. Aging will cease at about thirty years and diseases will no longer plague the general populace.

THE FACTORS WHICH CAUSE AGING AND DISEASE

ALL DISEASE IS THE RESULT OF A PARTIAL FAILURE
WITHIN THE INTELLIGENCE SYSTEM OF ANY ORGANISM.
Roger D. Blomquist: MYSTIC
Supraconsciousness Network, 2005

All biological entities and their components have built-in programming which manages their structure and function. We call this programming INTELLIGENCE. As long as this Intelligence is not compromised it will sustain its component's structure and functioning until the end of its allotted existence. The process works like this:

INTELLIGENCE➔STRUCTURE➔FUNCTION

Like the integrated circuits (IC's) in a computer the Intelligence required to generate and maintain a human vehicle is stored in pinhead sized units. There are twenty-seven such units for constructing and maintaining the physical and energy systems. These IC's, along with eight mental and eighteen emotional thoughtform IC's, are stored in the Solar Plexus. Their Intelligence partially programs the three matrices.

Referring to the Earthly Vehicle chart, Chi flows through the Subconscious CPU module and is programmed with Life Plan and karma Intelligence. It then absorbs the appropriate Factors from History and Genetic to construct a vehicle to complete the Life Plan successfully. This information then passes through the three matrices and ends up on the Etheric Circuit Board where it joins with Energy and System Intelligence to instruct the DNA how to construct the Vehicle.

DETRIMENTAL FACTORS—EXTRINSIC

The following factors may have a damaging effect on the Protégé during one or more of his/her five previous incarnations; their residual effects always influence the current life in subtle ways whether mental, emotional, or physical.

1. ENTITIES:

We are surrounded by spirit entities, the most common being earthbound Proteges who do not realize their vehicle has died. They often gather in churches, stores, and graveyards. Healers can remove them by requesting the Spirit Doctors to conduct them to their appropriate place in the Universe. Even more common are Activated Shells. When a human vehicle dies the Protégé departs immediately; the etheric, or energetic, body takes from two to four hours to leave the cadaver and begin to disintegrate. Pieces of this skeleton sometimes stick to living vehicles and interfere with their energy patterns. Spirit Doctors can dispose of them rapidly. Other common entities include Demon Spirits and devices and Energy Parasites.

2. HEX/CURSE:

A curse is intended to cause harm to someone immediately; a hex is usually cast on an individual to harm him and his descendants.

It takes an experienced magician to cast an effective hex today; however, a Master healer may occasionally stumble on one in the five History incarnations.

3. INFECTIONS, PARASITES, POISONS, TOXINS:

These common conditions are usually easy to diagnosis when they produce overt symptoms; however, even when their material stuff is eradicated or neutralized their energetic signatures remain and may lead to the development of strands, clusters, and loops much later in the incarnation.

4. TRAUMA:

Obviously, damage to the vehicle if severe enough will cause its death and the departure of the PROTÉGÉ in the current incarnation. The ill effects of lesser trauma may prompt statements such as: "He has never been the same since the accident, the operation, etc." Cell memories from previous incarnations will be covered in the next section.

DETRIMENTAL FACTORS—INTRINSIC

These factors originate within the entity but their roots may be in one or more preceding incarnations.

1. Destiny Factors: Karma and Life Plan

The history IC in the subconscious stores five incarnations. When the current incarnation ends it is archived and the oldest Incarnation is moved to the Protégé's Book of Life. These five lives may contain incidents which require resolution during the current life, and these learning experiences may include disease conditions. If and when the Karma and Life Plan requirements are satisfied these directives are not automatically deleted and may lead to a premature death of the vehicle. This is a design flaw which will be corrected in the Sixth Root Race. Journeyman healers can delete this obsolete material upon request.

2. Displacement:

This condition is a mis-alignment of the Etheric body to the flesh and blood vehicle. A bruise is a simple example. Since the etheric material is energetic a blow to the vehicle causes the physical and etheric to separate. If the blow is severe enough it will take a finite period of time for the separation to heal and, without the underlying energetic support, a bruise develops at the point of impact. In very severe accidents the separation may never heal naturally resulting in unusual symptoms.

Displacement can also develop due to the wear and tear of aging. It will then show up as a generalized condition interfering with the operation of most if not all systems. This overall creakiness also responds to a change in the weather.

3. Inflammation:

A localized physical condition in which part of the body becomes reddened, swollen, hot, and often painful, especially as a reaction to injury or infection.
The New Oxford American Dictionary

The Immune System
The tissues, organs, and physiological processes used by the body to identify a protein as abnormal or foreign and prevent it from harming the organism.
Taber's Cyclopedic Medical Dictionary, Edition 17
F. A. Davis Company, 1993

When the human vehicle suffers an injury, infection, poisoning, or any other threatening assault the immune system mobilizes to repel the invasion. This response varies with the attack, but when the enemy is overcome the immune system withdraws its forces and remains vigilant. The soldiers on the field of battle are known as antibodies.

But today, how did peanut butter become a menace to the vehicle?

Vaccination against childhood diseases became law around 1940. This was the biggest blunder ever instigated by Allopathic medicine.

Before vaccinations a pregnant woman created thousands of maternal antibodies and transferred them to her fetus to protect the newborn until his/her own immune system was sufficiently developed.

After vaccinations, and never having experienced childhood diseases as Nature intended, the new mother's immune system only generated 80% of the antibodies produced in the previous generation. And now, after four generations of vaccination, the mother's antibody count is down to about 30% of the optimum. Maternal antibodies were not designed to protect the newborn against childhood diseases, but they were designed to protect against just about anything else. Vaccination creates an antigen signaling that the disease has come and gone. The only thing missing is a couple of weeks education and training of an immature immune system.

A child's immune system matures at about five years. After four generations of vaccination the mother's decreased antibody supply is exhausted after only two years. This leaves the child unprotected from attack by germs, viruses, and even peanut butter. All the new allergies, and the development of all auto-immune diseases, can be traced to faulty training of the developing immune systems of children.

Faulty immune systems often fail to discontinue their attacks in the field (antibodies, blood flow, etc.) even when the crisis is over. The result is chronic inflammation which can only be resolved by replacing the worn out immune system Intelligence Modules and then correctly training these replacements.

4. Miasms:

ANY OF THE THREE UNDERLYING
CHRONIC DISEASES THAT AFFLICT
HUMANKIND: SYCOSIS, SYPHILLIS, AND PSORA.
Oxford American Dictionary

Samuel Hahnemann (1755-1843) was the developer of Homeopathy, a remedy based healing system. Working scientifically, he discovered miasms, a contamination of the DNA. The miasms listed above have been around since the days of the caveman. Over the millennia approximately sixty miasms have contaminated the human genetic pool, the latest being the Allopathic miasm caused by extensive chemical medication.

Children born with multiple miasms have a predilection to many disease conditions, sometimes appearing at birth or shortly thereafter.

Since miasms are primarily energetic in nature Master healers can detect their presence and remove them. However, they are sometimes employed as algorithms in Karma and Life Plan scenarios and cannot be deleted.

5. Multiple Personality Disorder:

The Invisible Friend: The newborn child is just that—new. The basic systems needed to sustain life are functional—everything else needs to experience and learn. Sometimes the child's visual system can temporarily see at a higher than normal frequency; this allows him/her to see earthbound spirits invisible to adults. Unless the child is truly clairvoyant this ability usually disappears by age six.

Multiple Personalities: This situation may be part of Karma or Life Plans. The child who is mistreated, bullied, or beaten may seem to retreat inwardly and present an alternate stronger persona when these things occur. Actually, the child's emotional state leaves him open to possession and an earthbound Protégé takes over the child's vehicle to protect him as much as possible. Unfortunately, a demon spirit in the vicinity might well do the same thing. The second Protégé will leave when the danger is over but the demon may or may not want to depart. Since what we call demon spirits are usually fallen angels they are not as dangerous as TV and movies depict. At the request of a Healer they can usually be arrested and removed by Deputy Spirit Doctors without a formal exorcism.

6. Signatures:

A SIGNATURE IS A DISTINCTIVE PATTERN,
PRODUCT, OR CHARACTERISTIC
BY WHICH SOMEONE OR SOMETHING CAN BE IDENTIFIED.
NEW OXFORD AMERICAN DICTIONARY

All perceptible matter is condensed energy as shown by Einstein's famous formula and the bomb which it fathered. Therefore, all matter will exhibit two signatures, one for its material component and one for its energetic origin. For example, radioactive materials give off an energy signature which can be detected by a Geiger counter and which can damage biological entities. Unfortunately, instrumentation is not yet available that is able to detect the energy signatures of common substances such as water, salt, and wood.

These energy signatures can accumulate in the flesh and blood vehicle and eventually give rise to physical symptoms. For example, the signature for alcohol accumulates in the Etheric Matrix and normally tends to dissipate in about six hours. In an alcoholic the signature gradually builds up because it is being frequently replenished. Eventually it spreads into the Emotional and Mental matrices and causes the personality to deteriorate.

Drugs, whether medical or recreational, have more complex signatures and tend to act the same way; however, their ill effects take longer to surface because of the small dosages employed.

7. Thoughtforms:

THOUGHTS ARE THINGS!

Intangibles such as sights, sounds, smells, emotions, and thoughts have their own characteristic energy signatures. Thoughts in particular, when repeated and sustained, are able to affect the human vehicle for good or for bad. This may be the origin of Mantras in Buddhist religious practices. Consider the following:

My dad died of a heart attack in his forties;
his father went the same way at the same age.
I'm forty-two so I guess it's my time to go.

Obsessing on a thought like this might cause it to infiltrate the Etheric Matrix and become a self-fulfilling prophecy.

The design of the human vehicle includes eight mental thoughtforms and eighteen emotional thoughtforms installed in the matrices. Of course, the learning experiences of life on Earth can cause damage to these insubstantial waveforms; and, as noted above, undesirable thoughtforms may invade the matrices and upset the balance of the entire structure. Mental or emotional disease may be the result of this damage.

8. Cell Memories:

The history IC on the CPU circuit board holds the Protégé's five previous incarnations; however, to save memory space only the most significant events are recorded. Memories of severe pain or death may trigger allergies, phobias, or physical symptoms difficult to diagnosis. Here is an example:

About a thousand years ago a forty year old
soldier is engaged in hand-to-
hand combat. An enemy sneaks up behind
him and cracks his head with an
axe. The soldier falls but does not die for several
agonizing hours. Fast forward to today. Now in
incarnation as a woman approaching forty the
Protégé's Mentor attempts to heal the old
trauma by triggering headaches
which have no apparent cause. Usually this
only happens when a healer
is available to delete the memory. In like manner fear of heights could
be traced back to a deadly fall, and an allergy to cats might be rooted
in a mauling by a tiger hundreds of years earlier.

CHAPTER FIVE

HEALING

The Path of the Healer

Healers are made, not born! Before embarking on the path of healing the complicated human vehicle the Protégé must successfully complete at least three incarnations repairing human vehicles. The first might be a tribal medicine man or woman many centuries ago; the second an apothecary in the 1700's; the third as a nurse during WW1. The possibilities are manifold, but these experiences are necessary before graduating to healing.

With that in mind let us treat healing as a craft with three levels:

Apprentice, Journeyman, Master. Keep in mind that to complete each level will probably require at least two incarnations.

It is necessary to point out the healer's place in the process. Because of the low frequency of the human vehicle the healer is unable to identify and control the subtle energies used to correct the patient's faulty patterns. Also, because of the mandatory amnesia associated with the incarnation process the aspiring healer will not remember all of the training he experienced in previous lifetimes. This was the case with our itinerant healer; however, he was born clairvoyant and was well trained in all seven of the Mystery Schools.

Considering these facts, the healer must be considered the intermediary between the patients and the Spirit Doctors who do the actual treatments.

The Apprentice Healer

The apprentice healer seems to be born with the "gift." They find out accidently that their touch and their empathy ease the ills of others. An individual without this gift but who seems successful is probably not on the Path and might well be a charlatan.

Depending on the Life Plan of the apprentice he or she could remain at this stage improving their technique, or they could make some progress by appropriate studies. In the West Therapeutic Touch is popular and Reiki from the East is now available.

Apprentice healing is limited to close contact because the healer is a conduit transferring energies supplied by Spirit Doctors to the patient. When Christ walked the Earth he primarily practiced apprentice style. But He also did some distant healing, the sign of the Journeyman, and many miraculous healings, the sign of a Master.

The Journeyman Healer

While there are 5000+ Apprentice healers now practicing on Earth there are only about 400 Journeyman presently in incarnation, and about 85 of them are masquerading as doctors. Many more are needed because of the increasing population and the general poor level of health of humanity. For the same reasons this book is intended for the development of distance healing. Such a healer can service many patients in a day without time spent traveling, and the patients can be located anywhere on Earth.

The Master Healer

At this point in time there are only seven Master healers in incarnation. Five of them rely on intuition, mental prompting from their Mentors, while the other two use dowsing to receive guidance. This seems like a good place to further investigate dowsing, an essential technique for the distant healer.

DOWSING

A technique for searching for underground water, minerals, or anything invisible, by observing the motion of a pointer ... or the changes in direction of a pendulum, supposedly in response to unseen influences.
The New Oxford American Dictionary, Third Edition

Dowsing has been successfully employed for thousands of years—and has been disparaged for the same time span. Essentially dowsing is highly developed intuition or "gut feeling." Every human being has a soul, a spiritual entity learning and evolving through its experiences in managing a flesh and blood vehicle. This earth-bound soul is the Protégé of a Mentor, a higher level spirit, perhaps even an ascended Master, who was assigned to guide his student intuitively through the incarnation. The Mentor is a member of what the Huna call "Poe Aumakua," or the Great Company of High Selves, an association of all the entities involved in Project Earth.

When an earth-bound soul seeks direction it often comes intuitively; however, if dowsing is a part of the human's Life Plan his Mentor will be able, with sufficient practice on the Protégé's part, to control a device such as a pendulum using the Protégé's nervous system. Thus, the Mentor is able to supply the inquiring Protégé with answers to his or her questions.

Pendulum dowsing is usually done by the Socratic method in reverse. The student asks questions which can only be answered "Yes or No." Begin by drawing a large plus sign. The vertical line is YES like a nod of the head, the horizontal NO like a shake. Mark the lines appropriately. Hold your pendulum steady over the center point and verbally command it to swing along the YES line; make no attempt to move it. Repeat with the NO line. It may take some practice to achieve the proper response because you are training your nervous system to reply to your Mentor's thought.

Next command your pendulum to rotate clockwise; this is similar to the "working" icon which is often displayed on a computer startup.

When these exercises show some progress start asking simple questions with Y&N answers. Follow with finding things which have been misplaced. The possibilities are unlimited, but keep in mind that the accuracy of your answers depends on the accuracy of your questions!

With dedicated practice there will come a time when the communication between Mentor and Protégé will become smooth and effortless, like two old friends conversing. Indeed, there will come a time when, in your healing work, your Mentor will actually prompt the needed questions intuitively.

CHAPTER SIX

TREATMENT

IF YOU ABIDE IN ME, AND MY
WORDS ABIDE IN YOU, ASK FOR
WHATEVER YOU WISH, AND IT
WILL BE DONE FOR YOU.
JOHN 15: 7

Our itinerant healer/preacher of two thousand years ago left us with many words of wisdom. It is unfortunate that he is not here today to translate his thoughts from the original Aramaic into English. However, the following is an accurate interpretation of the above:

Ask and you shall receive.
Seek and you shall find.
Knock and the door shall be opened to you.

Basically, the thinking and questioning mind will eventually be rewarded by achieving the object of its quest. With regard to healing the object of the quest is to restore the health of a human vehicle so that its Protégé soul can complete the Plan of the incarnation successfully. It is futile to attempt to restore a vehicle to perfect health because that would possibly be interfering with Destiny. However, true healing will generally improve the overall health of the patient because it restores the functioning of the underlying energetics.

Here it must be said that the Healer's path to Mastery takes a minimum of five incarnations; however, these incarnations are never strung together but are interspersed with excursions into other fields of endeavor in order to develop a well-rounded psyche. With that in mind let us proceed to an analysis of the basic healing technique which can be used successfully by any healer.

ANY SUFFICIENTLY ADVANCED TECHNOLOGY IS
INDISTINGUISHABLE FROM MAGIC.
Arthur C. Clarke

The healer must follow these basic steps:

1. QUIET THOUGHTS AS IN MEDITATION.

Because healing requires the assistance of Beings who dwell in the LIGHT (the Sun) the mind of the healer must span 93 million miles in order to communicate with his/her Guides. The Mental Energy Spectrum operates in the same manner as the Electromagnetic Spectrum: the lower the frequency the longer the wavelength. The ideal center brainwave frequency is 2 Hertz, Theta or light sleep level, which clears the static of random thoughts from the brain and allows the mind to roam the Solar System. To achieve this state the Healer should schedule his treatment sessions as a monk would schedule his meditations or a musician his practice periods. Also, helpful would be a few moments of chanting AUM, the basic resonant frequency of the Cosmos.

2. CONTACT YOUR GUIDE.

SO SHALL MY WORD BE THAT GOETH
FORTH OUT OF MY MOUTH;
IT SHALL NOT RETURN UNTO ME VOID, BUT
IT SHALL ACCOMPLISH THAT WHICH I PLEASE,
AND IT SHALL PROSPER IN THE THING
WHERETO I SENT IT.
Isaiah 55: 11

Planet Earth is the only location in the entire Cosmos where meaningful communication is achieved by the spoken word!

A Mentor is not allowed to read his Protégé's mind but he is able to see and hear when his student needs or requests assistance. Because of the mandatory amnesia inherent in the incarnation procedure the Mentor can only guide his Protégé along his predetermined Life Plan by intuitive hints or "gut feelings." (Note that the Life Plan cannot be considered predestination because the Protégé agreed to follow it prior to starting the incarnation. But because of the mandatory amnesia he or she does not remember this contract.) Finally, when communicating with your Mentor be sure to work in private lest you be led away in restraints.

If you do not know your Mentor's name you can work it out by dowsing; otherwise, assign him or her a name which seems appropriate.

3. IDENTIFY YOUR PATIENT.

THIS WORD IS SPOKEN FOR THE ENTITY KNOWN AS
(JOHN SMITH.)

This statement introduces the patient not only to the Healer's Mentor but also to the Great Company of High Selves. In most cases the interaction of healer and patient is prearranged and the Spirit Doctors are already aware of the patient's condition.

4. INITIATE THE TREATMENT.

STATEMENT ONE

I DECLARE THAT THE HEALTH OF (JOHN
SMITH'S) VEHICLE IS PERFECT!
AMEN!

Hold this thought until you sense the treatment is over; if using a pendulum, it should indicate "working" by circling clockwise. The AMEN releases the request to the spirit realm and is like hitting "Enter" or "Return" on your computer.

This declaration is a request for a miracle, and sometimes a miracle happens. Each request phrased in this manner is considered by the Silent Watchers and either fulfilled by them or rerouted to the appropriate level of the hierarchy for processing. Either way, it begins the healing procedure by initiating the flow of Chihan to the patient and by mobilizing the first team of Spirit Doctors.

This declaration should not be repeated for this patient. Sudden miracles are very rare and it may take several days for any noticeable improvement in the patient's condition to appear. Check with your MENTOR daily to see if and when to proceed to the next step.

At this point feedback from the patient/family becomes useful.

To keep things simple offer only three choices: the patient is better, the same, or worse. And inform those involved that the recovery period is proportional to the time span of the illness.

5. CONTINUE TREATMENT, FACTORS

Repeat steps 1, 2, and 3 if necessary.

STATEMENT TWO

I WANT ALL THE INTRINSIC AND
EXTRINSIC FACTORS CAUSING
(JOHN SMITH'S) AILMENTS TO BE
PURGED FROM HIS HISTORY!
AMEN!

This statement instructs the Spirit Doctors to remove all obsolete and unnecessary FACTORS from the patient's Subconscious CPU and from the three matrices. This is like unclogging a drain—it allows the atmospheric healing energies to flow freely through the vehicle. Again, check daily with your MENTOR on the patient's condition and if and when to proceed to the next step.

6. CONTINUE TREATMENT, PHYSICAL SYSTEMS

Repeat steps 1, 2, and 3 if necessary.

STATEMENT THREE

I WANT ALL OF (JOHN SMITH'S) FLESH
AND BLOOD AILMENTS
TO BE HEALED AS RAPIDLY AS POSSIBLE!
AMEN!

Approximately sixty percent of a healer's patients, those with less serious ailments, will recover soon after treatment. Others facing a longer convalescence may benefit from accelerated healing techniques. This request mobilizes the Spirit Doctors who specialize in dense physical repairs to initiate such treatments.

Keep on mind that you, the healer, are also on a path of learning. When a patient does not make the expected progress it will be up to you to investigate more deeply into his/her history in order to find the blockage and remove it. One useful method is to start at birth and proceed through each year until a detrimental factor is detected. The first such factor is usually the start of a strand, cluster, or loop which manifests many years later as serious symptoms.

Also note that STATEMENTS TWO & THREE are generic and can be re-worded to apply to specific circumstances and conditions.

If the patient exhibits little or no improvement we must assume one of three possibilities:

1. He may be approaching the end of the incarnation.

2. There may be active Life Plan or Karma obligations still needing to be satisfied.

3. There may be significant FLESH AND BLOOD problems requiring resolution.

Item #1 is outside the realm of healing. The item #2 timeframe can usually be shortened if it is close to completion. Item #3 can usually be healed.

This three-phase treatment schedule was developed in the Third Root Race and has been updated as the human vehicle has evolved.

IN CONCLUSION

This completes the basic treatments of 21st Century Healing.

Many will say it is identical to 1st century healing, and they would be absolutely correct. The only thing that has changed is that a simple procedure, long obscured by mysticism and materialism, can now be actually explained and simplified by the advances of materialism.

Can these techniques be used successfully by atheists and agnostics? Doubtful! However, over the centuries medicine men, magicians, and other such practitioners have relied on the assistance of spirit helpers to control weather, to assure an ample food supply, and to heal injury and illness.

But in this scientific age most of the well-known healers who have written books about their techniques give the impression that they personally accumulate subtle energies and pass them on to their patients. This may be true in some instances, especially in contact healing sessions; however, the demands of distance healing require the assistance of mobile and knowledgeable helpers to achieve the desired results.

The Spirit Doctor corps was created in the Third Root Race to assist the developing human vehicles. Since humanity was planned to learn and progress by experience the SD's primary rule of engagement has been and still is: Do not intervene unless asked!

And one very important final thought:

WE LEARN SOMETHING BY DOING IT.
THERE IS NO OTHER WAY.
John Holt

CHAPTER SEVEN
1st CENTURY HEALING

If the reader has reached this point he or she might well be asking: What do I do now? It all depends on where you are now.

If you are happy and satisfied with your work in healing you are probably following your life plan. One of the happiest persons I know repairs our automobiles and really enjoys his work. And he is making a good living at it. He is scheduled to repair human vehicles in his next incarnation.

If you are already helping to restore peoples' health you may be an apprentice healer. If your work is always very good to outstanding, if the patients improve rapidly, and if you enjoy what you doing—these are indications that you are applying healing energies along with standard treatments—then you are probably at the apprentice level already.

If you apply healing energies to your patients, whether unknowingly as a doctor or knowingly as a practicing contact healer, and your results are consistently excellent, you can be considered a journeyman.

Analyze your situation and decide if you fit one of these descriptions, or are a true beginner willing to start on the path of the healer. The starting point is the TREATMENT chapter and your first and most important patient is yourself. The human vehicle is so complex that there is always something that is not quite right. (Note that you can change the STATEMENT wording to apply to specific conditions.) Start with some minor nuisance problem that never seems to go away and proceed to other more complicated symptoms. After following the TREATMENT procedure carefully, and after a number of attempts, if there is no improvement you may not be destined to be a healer in this incarnation. However, if all goes well covertly expand your realm of distant healing to relatives and friends.

Let's face it: Healing requires practice. To allow sufficient practice the rule of the patient having to "ask for healing" is suspended for novices. Observe those close to you and note their health complaints. You may or may not inform them of your activities. Return to the TREATMENT chapter and review the procedure carefully. Quieting the mind and speaking aloud are essential. Working with one patient and one symptom, re-word STATEMENTS TWO & THREE to fit the situation. Then proceed through all three STATEMENTS pausing between them and trying to sense intuitively when to move to the next one. If dowsing, watch your pendulum.

It may take a finite period of time for results to appear. Observe and question your patient--Is he or she is feeling better? You may be surprised by sudden improvements. If things go well proceed to the Basic Analysis, the first step in the healing process as it was done in the 1st CENTURY by the first documented Master Healer.

Healing is perfectly safe. The worst that can happen is that nothing happens.

BASIC ANALYSIS

Thus, when a disease on the periphery like a skin eruption, colitis or an arthritic condition is given the wrong treatment, it retreats to the more essential organs or the deeper emotional and mental planes.
George Vithoulkas: A New Model of Health and Disease
North Atlantic Books, 1991

There are a number of ways to pinpoint the cause of a symptom or disease. We will call the first such cause, the first glitch in the human computer, the ROOT CAUSE. It was noted in HEALING that the human vehicle is the most complex entity ever created and that this complexity leads to the formation of strands, clusters, and loops. The ROOT CAUSE is the initial fault which eventually results in diseases and aging. And it generally occurs during the first ten years of the incarnation.

Since we exist in a cause and effect environment you might well ask: Where does the ROOT CAUSE come from? The ROOT CAUSE is the agent of your Destiny! IT, along with the intuitions, dreams, and conscience supplied by your Mentor, attempts to balance your Karma and to keep you on the path to complete your Life Plan successfully.

Current medical science cannot detect and correct the ROOT CAUSE. It is often energetic in nature, the invisible remains of a trauma or illness which was apparently completely healed. Any EXTRINSIC or INTRINSIC FACTOR could be a ROOT CAUSE. Unfortunately, when the ROOT CAUSE completes its work it is not automatically deleted. This design flaw will be corrected by the Seventh Root Race.

When Christ walked the Earth He and the Spirit Doctors were able to detect and repair ROOT CAUSES thereby collapsing of all the strands, clusters, and loops which developed from this initial defect. And this was the secret behind His hundreds of successful healings some of which were truly miraculous. Just as we can experience a cascade failure, healers can trigger a cascade healing.

WORKING WITH THE 'ROOT CAUSE'

Can a novice healer work with this preliminary information and do successful healing? Yes!

Does a novice healer have to identify the ROOT CAUSE? No, but it would certainly help. The identity of the ROOT CAUSE can invariably be found in FACTORS.

Begin by asking a few questions about the patient:

1. Does this person's vehicle harbor a ROOT CAUSE?
2. At what age did the ROOT CAUSE occur?

3. What FACTOR is the ROOT CAUSE?

4. At this time is it appropriate to rectify the undesirable effects of the ROOT CAUSE?

Note the answers and proceed to treatment.

Treatment for ROOT CAUSE follows the same procedure as outlined earlier but with changes in the STATEMENT wording. Review steps 1 through 4 in the TREATMENT chapter. Then proceed with:

5. CONTINUE TREATMENT-- ROOT CAUSE

I WANT THE ROOT CAUSE TO BE PURGED FROM (JOHN SMITH'S) VEHICLE AND THE STRANDS, CLUSTERS, AND LOOPS WHICH IT ENGENDERED TO BE DESTROYED! AMEN!

As usual, wait for your pendulum to stop circling or your intuition to sense completion of the procedure.

Note that no method of healing is 100% successful. DESTINY has complete control over the Protégé's existence during his or her sojourns on Earth, and any attempt to alter DESTINY is futile! Your best resource is to develop a working relationship with your Mentor. To aid you on your own quest here are some alternate methods of patient analysis, and some STATEMENT words which may be appropriate in certain situations.

1. ROOT CAUSE

2. DISEASE/SYMPTOM:

   MENTAL, EMOTIONAL, PHYSICAL

3. INCARNATION (0)

   STRANDS, CLUSTERS, LOOPS

4. HISTORY INCARNATIONS

   PLUS INCARNATION (0)

STRANDS, CLUSTERS, LOOPS

5. THOUGHTFORMS

6. MECHANICAL DAMAGE

2. TREATMENT COMMANDS

ABOLISH

DELETE

DESTROY

EXCISE

PURGE

REMOVE

TRANSMUTE

EDUCATE

REJUVINATE

REGENERATE

REPAIR

REPLACE

RESTORE

AFTERWORD

In this little book I may seem to have been somewhat critical of the medical profession. There are many dedicated individuals working as doctors, nurses, and aides; however, it is unfortunate that Allopathic Medicine throughout its history has been enamored of scientific materialism and vigorously opposed to any competition no matter how promising it appears. This symptom-squashing style of medicine has put forth and tried many heroic treatments, some with disastrous results for the patients involved. This continues today with a constant search for "Magic Bullets" of dubious effectiveness, high cost, and serious side effects.

The main reason for this situation is not a lack of dedication among the "toilers in the field" but because the field itself has become too involved with pharmaceutical and equipment manufacturers and insurance companies. The result is the current medical Juggernaut which is insatiably devouring the economic systems of many civilized countries without really healing those who seek its help.

Albert Einstein, although not a mystic, proved that matter is a condensed form of energy. Therefore, the human physical vehicle, since it is made of matter, must also be condensed energy. But condensing flawed energy results in defective matter. Since manipulating physical matter medically does not correct the underlying energy faults true healing can only occur when the energy patterns are properly restored.

Perhaps this little volume will have a "Butterfly Effect," not by triggering a hurricane, but by clearing the skies and allowing the "Essential Simplicity" of spiritually based healing to shine through.

Thanks for your time and attention!

Bob Bendykowski

APPENDIX

THE HUMAN VEHICLES ETHERIC CIRCUIT BOARD

SYSTEM INTELLIGENCE MODULES:

1) Cosmic Interface
2) Subconscious CPU, Matrices
3) History
4) Destiny
5) Genetic
6) Core
7) Major Chakras
8) Minor Chakras
9) Spleen Chakras, Meridian System, Nadis
10) Aura
11) CNS, ANS, Plexi
12) Cardio, Blood
13) DNA
14) Endocrine
15) Exocrine
16) Gastro-Intestinal
17) Genital, Urinary
18) Immune
19) Muscular
20) Respiratory, Lymphatic
21) Joints
22) Skeleton
23) Aural
24) Visual
25) Touch, Skin
26) Taste
27) Smell

THOUGHTFORMS

MENTAL THOUGHTFORMS:

1) ATTENTION
2) BALANCE
3) BROADMINDEDNESS
4) COMPOSURE
5) ACUITY
6) PRAISE
7) PRUDENCE
8) SELF-REALIZATION

EMOTIONAL THOUGHTFORMS:

1)	AFFECTION	10)	ENDURANCE
2)	APPRECIATION	11)	ALTRUISM
3)	RESPECTFULNESS	12)	ACCEPTANCE
4)	CALM	13)	ONE-POINTEDNESS
5)	CHARITY	14)	PERSEVERANCE
6)	GRACIOUSNESS	15)	SELF-RELIANCE
7)	COMMITMENT	16)	SPIRITUALITY
8)	CONCENTRATION	17)	STRENGTH
9)	FORGIVENESS	18)	COMPASSION

ETHERIC THOUGHTFORMS: GO TO NAMED DISEASES

DETRIMENTAL FACTORS

EXTRINSIC:	INTRINSIC:	ENTITIES:
ENTITIES	CELL MEMORIES	AS: ACTIVATED SHELLS
HEX/CURSE	DESTINY FACTORS	DD: DEMON DEVICES
INFECTIONS	DISPLACEMENT	DS: DEMON SPIRITS
PARASITES	INFLAMMATION	EB: EARTHBOUNDS
POISONS/ TOXINS	MIASMS	EP: ENERGY PARASITES
TRAUMA	MPD—DID	HA: HUMAN ARTIFICIALS
OTHER	SIGNATURES	OTHER
	THOUGHTFORMS	
	OTHER	

ENTITIES

If you don't believe in angels you probably don't believe in any other types of entities. But we are surrounded by a multitude of invisible beings.

Keep in mind that the average person's range of vision is very limited. Clairvoyants are born with the ability to see higher frequencies. Drugs such as LSD alter human optics to detect higher, good trip, or lower, bad trip, apparitions.

The human vehicle is protected from entity invasion by its aura, an invisible shield of both firm and fluffy fibers emanating from the skin. If the aura deteriorates the vehicle is left open to intrusion by entities. Drug and alcohol addicts are particularly susceptible to this occurrence. In the late 1980's I worked with an addiction counselor who supplied me with the names of about 150 of her clients. At my request Spirit Doctors removed their intruders and relocated them to appropriate places in the universe. The counselor retired with a remarkable record of achievement.

Entities which successfully invade a human vehicle can drain its energy and eventually upset its mental, emotional, and physical systems. If you have unusual or intractable symptoms or lack of progress in healing the cause may be entity involvement. It might be a good practice to check for entities before beginning the formal treatments.

BIBLIOGRAPHY

Allen, D. S. & Deliar, J. B.: Cataclysm!
Bear & Company, 1997

Blomquist, Roger D., MD: MYSTIC
Supraconsciousness Network, 2005

Citro, Massimo: The Basic Code of the Universe
Park Street Press, 2011

Easwaran, Eknath (translator): The Bhagavad Gita
Nilgiri Press, 1985

Edwards, Harry: A Guide to the Understanding and
Practice of Spiritual Healing

The Healer Publishing Company Limited, 1974

Hall, Manley Palmer: Healing—The Divine Art
Philosophical Research Society, 1944

Holmes, Ernest: The Science of Mind
G. P. Putnam's Sons: 1988

King, Serge Kahili: Healing for the Millions
Hunaworks, 2004

Lao Tzu (Brian Walker, translator): Tao Te Ching
St. Martin's Griffin, 1995

Leichtman, Robert & Japikse, Carl: Working With Angels
Enthea Press, 1992

Leviton, Richard: Physician
    Hampton Roads, 2000

Modi, Shakuntala, MD: Memories of God and Creation
    Hampton Roads, 2000

Newton, Michael: Journey of Souls
    Llewellyn Publications, 2000

The New Oxford American Dictionary
    Third Edition, 2010

Oxford American Writer's Thesaurus
    Third Edition, 2012

Pearl, Eric: The Reconnection
    Hay House, Ins., 2001

Powell, A. E.: The Etheric Double
    Quest Books, 1960

Tansley, David: Radionics and the Subtle Anatomy of Man
    C. W. Daniel, 1972

Three Initiates: The Kybalion
    Yogi Publication Society, 1912

THE TORAH
    The Jewish Publication Society, 1962

Virtue, Doreen, Ph.D.: Archangels & Ascended Masters
    Hay House, Inc., 2003

Vithoulkas, George: A New Model of Health and Disease
    North Atlantic Books, 1991

Yogananda, Paramahansa: Autobiography of a Yogi
    Self-Realization Fellowship, 1946

Printed in the United States
By Bookmasters